A 10-Day Practical Step by Step -

Financial Freedom Through Investing.

LANCE KNIGHT

Text Copyright © Lance Knight

All rights reserved. No part of this guide may be reproduced in any form without permission in writing from the publisher except in the case of brief quotations embodied in critical articles or reviews.

Legal & Disclaimer

The information contained in this book and its contents is not designed to replace or take the place of any form of medical or professional advice; and is not meant to replace the need for independent medical, financial, legal or other professional advice or services, as may be required. The content and information in this book has been provided for educational and entertainment purposes only.

The content and information contained in this book has been compiled from sources deemed reliable, and it is accurate to the best of the Author's knowledge, information and belief. However, the Author cannot guarantee its accuracy and validity and cannot be held liable for any errors and/or omissions. Further, changes are periodically made to this book as and when needed. Where appropriate and/or necessary, you must consult a professional (including but not limited to your doctor, attorney, financial advisor or such other professional advisor) before using any of the suggested remedies, techniques, or information in this book.

Upon using the contents and information contained in this book, you agree to hold harmless the Author from and against any damages, costs, and expenses, including any legal fees potentially resulting from the application of any of the information provided by this book. This disclaimer applies to any loss, damages or injury caused by the use and application, whether directly or indirectly, of any advice or information presented, whether for breach of contract, tort, negligence, personal injury, criminal intent, or under any other cause of action.

You agree to accept all risks of using the information presented inside this book.

You agree that by continuing to read this book, where appropriate and/or necessary, you shall consult a professional (including but not limited to your doctor, attorney, or financial advisor or such other advisor as needed) before using any of the suggested remedies, techniques, or information in this book.

Table of Contents

INTRODUCTION 4
CHAPTER 1: WHAT IS THE STOCK MARKET AND HOW DOES IT WORK? 6
CHAPTER 2: LEARN A FEW STOCK INVESTMENT BASICS BEFORE INVESTING YOUR MONEY.......7
CHAPTER 3: STOCK ORDER 9
CHAPTER 4: IPO AND WHY IS IT IMPORTANT? 12
CHAPTER 5: THE DIFFERENT TYPES OF OPTIONS 13
CHAPTER 6: GUIDELINE TO A GREAT STOCK INVESTMENT...................................14
CHAPTER 7: TRADE EXIT 15
CHAPTER 8: IMPORTANT STOCK TRADING TOOLS..17
CHAPTER 9: DOUBLE YOUR MONEY IN THE STOCK MARKET 19
CHAPTER 10: THE IMPORTANCE OF TRADING PSYCHOLOGY 21
CHAPTER 11: COMMON INVESTING MISTAKES BEGINNERS MAKE 23
CONCLUSION 25

Introduction

Thank you for downloading this book "**Investing**". I hope it gives you the direction to finding and making the right investment choice. Here are the key things you need to study right from the start, money management, your psychology, chart reading, the price action of your instrument of choice to work in, and how to quantify supply and demand properly. Do not spend all your time studying or worrying about the things you can't control and only do what you know to be true. The risk in investing and trading is unavoidable you get paid to take the risk, so take it, just make sure you have a plan to control it!

All I can tell you is that you need to be prepared and on point when you go into the live market. There are professional people in there that will walk over dead bodies to get paid and make money and all of them have a "kill everyone" mentality I assure you. They don't care if you lose all your money to them. It is nothing personal. They don't know you, so it is just business as usual in the market every day, and they are experts at their business, you hearing me now?

You need to do the education and training required and take the proper amount of time developing your rule-based plan. You also need to have yourself completely under control before ever stepping foot into the live market with your hard earned real money. To do it any other way is like playing Russian roulette with a completely loaded revolver. You can't win and will get FUBAR!

To be consistently successful over the long term you have to at least occasionally have the big winning trade. That is done on the daily or higher time frame chart. The biggest money and the "easiest" money are made outside the intraday timeframe. I know you probably won't listen to me, and you will day trade to start off however if you find yourself losing money in the very beginning maybe just refer to this section of this book and perhaps re-read it.

It doesn't matter if it is the equities market, Forex or futures, the news is always being reported just the opposite of what you should be doing the trading industry and the smart money guide the sheep of the herd with information herd techniques. As I said it is called information herding, and it goes on more than you know as a beginner. The media and the trading industry count on brand new traders and investors not doing their due diligence (DD) and making the mistake of buying high and selling low.

One of the worst mistakes any investor or trader can make is to trade on news or a tip from someone whose brother in law made a killing on a tip he got from someone else on XYZ companies stock. Might work once if you get lucky however most likely what will happen is you will lose all of your money on the position.

The talking heads on the TV get paid to say what they are saying about XYZ companies stock doing this or that. Think about that logically for a moment if you will. What are the talking heads saying, where is the price of the stock?

If the news is good, the stock is most likely approaching a high-level supply value area where the smart money and professionals are getting ready to sell from the unsuspecting retail of the herd traders who have been conditioned to buy high and are buying at the top of a move in PA.

On the flip side if the news is the bad price is most likely approaching a high-level demand value area where again the smart money and professionals are prepared to buy from the retail traders who are making their same mistakes over and over again by selling low where demand out weighs supply.

Chapter 1: What is the Stock Market and How Does it Work?

We all hear news about the stock market every day, we all know whether it is up or down, whether it has had a good or bad day, week or month. We all know fortunes can be made, or lost on it. But how many of us truly know what it is and how it works? The development of personal computers has resulted in more and more people investing their money, from home, in the markets. If you want to become an investor, it is important, therefore, to train in the art of trading. To be an effectual investor, you must learn the basics of the stock market.

The very first stock market dates back to the 17th when the Amsterdam Stock Exchange first introduced and pioneered continuous trade. This included short selling, options trading, debt-equity swaps and merchant banking. Nowadays, virtually every developed economy in the world have their stock market.

So, how do these markets work? Stocks are the means through which companies can raise money. Simply put: Stocks are the shares of a company that the owners sell to raise capital. When you own stock, you own a part of the company. A dividend on a share is that share's portion of the company's profits. For example, if the company has ten owners, and it makes a profit of $100,000 in the year, each owner would receive $10,000. The dividends are usually paid yearly.

The value of the share (or stock) will go up or down depending on how the value of the company fluctuates. However, if the stocks go below what you paid for them, you will not loose money unless you sell your stocks at that price. You may well recover from the paper losses when (and if) the value of the stock rebounds. However, always keep in mind that stocks do NOT offer a guaranteed return. You must choose them carefully. Having some degree of knowledge is important.

The companies that wish to sell shares must be publicly held. This means they must allow investors (people like you and me) to buy their stocks through an open market. The stock market is that open market. There are two main reasons for a company to want to sell shares. It is the way for a company to raise capital (money) to achieve its objectives, such s expansions and improvements, without having to borrow the money. Shares may also be sold when the owners want to reduce their holdings in the company and generate cash for their private use.

Each stock is usually traded on just one of the stock markets. The stock market or index is the Dow Jones Industrial Average. Only 30 stocks are part of this exchange! Therefore, you could be trading in many, many stocks and never be directly affected by how the Dow Jones is doing. The Dow Jones is well-known because it is where one would find the stock of the major companies.

The stock market consists of two markets, the primary and secondary markets. The primary market is where the first sale of shares by a company, at a base price, would take place. The secondary market, and most familiar, is where stock from publicly held companies is traded. Most investors tend to trade through a broker, however, more and more, people are learning about the stock market and doing their trading.

Chapter 2: Learn a Few Stock Investment Basics before Investing Your Money

The stock market is a livid place and has a considerable amount of movements every day. This variable nature of the stock market is one reason why people go for other forms of investment. However, those who do understand how to crack this puzzle can get fairly good results for their investments. There are some stock investment basics that you must learn or practice for safeguarding your investments.

Safe stock investment fundamentals for your assets

Now that you have decided to invest your not to easily earned money in stock exchange where market keeps fluctuating entire day, what are those stock investment basics that you must adopt to make wise decisions while investing in stocks,

Don't make a forecast market movement

At times, you will see various changes in the economic environment of the national and international market, which may look to you like a great index for the stock market. However, this may happen but not according to the effect you would have anticipated or for the stocks that you have invested for. For the umpteenth times, market pundits have read, estimated and suggested that calculating market changes in the connotation of your reading is merely doing too much, which may cause you heavy financial loss.

Holding stocks for avoiding heavy taxation

Tax is a contribution of every responsible citizen and therefore even when you earn from your market stocks you are eligible to pay government taxes, however with a wise decision, you can earn a waiver from heavy taxes. If you keep stocks for a period of one year or more, you taxation rates are much cheaper. But, if you are a frequent buyer and seller of stocks, you will pay higher tax rates.

Diversify your investments

According to many investment pundits, it is wise to keep the doors open for various types of investment. Apart from keeping track of stock picks for today in BSE, you must keep options open for investment in assets like house, land, gold, etc. In other options, you can explore in bonds cash, fixed bank deposits, recurring deposits, etc. Each of these options has a good returns and with a very low relevance to the instability of the market.

These are some of the very good stock investment basics which you can implement in your investment practices. It is always good to diversify the investment options, so that loss in any single investment doesn't affect you badly.

Chapter 3: Stock Order

If we want to take charge of our finances by trading in the stock market, or if we want to use an internet-based broker to trade with our money, it is important to know exactly what stock orders are.

Orders are the instructions customers will give their brokers (or electronic broker) to buy or sell stock on the exchange. There are some different orders, which allow us to have tighter control over the transactions we make. They can be very simple or complicated, and they can restrict the transaction either by price or by time.

Market or Open Order - This is the simplest and, most likely, the cheapest of the orders and it is the instruction to trade stock immediately at the current market prices, no matter what that price is.

Limit Order - This is the instruction which tells your broker to buy a security at not more, or sells at not less, than a specified price. In other words, you tell your broker the amount you want to sell for, or the amount you want to buy for, it is a fixed price order. Be aware that you might have to pay a higher commission to place this order than a Market Order, so it may make more financial sense just to place a simple Market Order.

Buy Limit Order - This is the instruction that a buy order can only be executed at the limit price or lower.

Sell Limit Order - This is the instruction that a sell order can only be executed at the limit price or higher.

Good-Till-Cancelled Order (GTC) - This is the order which is used in conjunction with other orders, and it instructs your broker to keep the order active until you cancel it. It is a specific canceling order, and some brokers may have limits on how long you can keep a Good-Till-Cancelled order open.

Day Order - The contrary of Good-Till-Cancelled Order and the most common of all the Orders. A Day Order is a market order that is in force from the time it is submitted until the time the market closes.

Immediate-Or-Cancel Order (IOC) - This is the instruction to cancel immediately an order. These orders allow for partial fills, which means they can instruct to cancel immediately a part of the order, it does not have to be the whole order.

Fill-Or-Kill Order (FOK) - These are normally limit orders that must be canceled immediately, and they require the full quantity of the order to be executed.

Stop Loss Order - This is an order to buy or sell a security. This works in the following way, your broker will place a stop order at a point below the market price at that time, in the event that the stock falls to the stop order level, the stop order will become a market order, and the broker will sell the stock. This order protects you against losses. Different types of Stop Orders fulfill different instructions. Buy-Stop Order will be used to limit a loss on a short sale. The buy stop price will always be above the current market price. A Sell-Stop Order will instruct to sell at the best available price after the price goes below the stop price. A Stop-Limit Order combines a Stop Order and a Limit Order, once the stop price is reached, the Stop-Limit Order becomes a Limit Order to buy or sell at the pre-specified limit price.

Trailing Stop Order – Though similar to Stop Orders, trailing Stop Orders function is to protect your profits. The Trailing Stop Order is entered with a stop parameter, such as a percentage change or the rise or fall in the security price. When the parameter is reached, the trailing stop order will turn into a market order to sell the stock. For example, if the trailing order is set at $1.00, the market order will be activated when the stock falls by $1.00. However, if the stock rises, the Trailing Order will follow it up, only becoming a market order if it falls by $1.00, or whichever parameter is chosen. There are a few variations of Trailing Stop Orders. Trailing Stop Limit Order, this is like the Trailing Order However instead of becoming a Market Order when triggered, this order becomes a Limit Order. Trailing Stop Trailing Limit Order is the most flexible possible order.

One Cancel Other Order - This is an order used when the trader wants to capitalize on one of two or more possible trades. This order will be composed of two parts giving a set of instructions each, whichever instruction is reached first, it would be carried out, and the other instruction would be canceled.

All of these orders can also be placed on the Electronic Markets. However, the Electronic Markets have rules which state the priority of the different orders. Market Orders have the highest priority, followed by Limit Orders. Therefore those are the orders preferred in the Electronic Markets.

Chapter 4: IPO and Why is it important?

IPO means Initial Public Offering. This is a company's first sale of stock to the general public.

In the late 1990s, with the stock market boom, there seemed to be a new IPO every week, making people rich overnight. After the stock market bubble burst in 2000, the IPO have become less common, but there still are some coming to the market every year. There not is visible as they were in the 1990s but they still can make you a good profit if you know where to find them!

IPOs become available when a company decides to sell, for the very first time, some of their stock to the general public, to raise funds to benefit the company.

The company will hire a brokerage firm to handle its initial public offering. They can use one or more brokerage firms, and these firms will be responsible for selling the stock to the public. Each of these brokerage firms will have a certain number of shares to sell. The brokerage firms will produce a brochure of the company. It will state the history, financial and workforce information as well as other details of the company. They will use this brochure as a sales tool to interest investors into buying the shares.

The brokerage firms' first port of call will be the cash-laden institutional investors, such as mutual funds, hedge funds, and pension funds. Then they will target those wealthy clients who can afford to buy large chunks of the shares. These two sets of clients will pay the 'offering price' for the shares. This is the price which the company and brokerage firms decide the shares should be sold for. In theory the 'offering price' is also the price at which the shares will be sold on the first day of trading, however, it does not always work out that way.

It is on that first day of trading that the general public has the chance to buy the stock for the first time. So, as you can see, the private investor is at the bottom of the pile when it comes to getting their hands on IPOs. If you want a chance at buying IPOs, you ought to consider joining a brokerage firm. However, before you dive feet first, you must do some research, ask the brokerage firm some questions, like if they offer IPOs, how much money do you have to invest, and how many transactions you have to carry out to be eligible to invest in IPOs.

A final warning, although money can be made quickly from a successful IPO, please know that they can be very high-risk transactions. They are a speculative stock as they are brand new and have no track record. Therefore, if you are going to invest in an IPO, it is important that you choose the right one. You must do your research and only invest if the company offering the IPO is constantly in the business news or it is a well-known company. Do not just go for the first IPO you see? Take your time, do your research and make sure that when you choose to invest in an IPO, it is with your eyes wide open, having done all the homework beforehand.

Chapter 5: The Different Types of Options

An option is an agreement between two parties concerning the buying or selling of an asset at a set price before a set date. Before we look at the different types of options available, let us quickly glance at the information an option contract should contain.

The first thing the option contract should specify is if the option holder holds the right to buy (call option) or right to sell (put Option). Another important piece of information is the quantity of the underlying asset. By this, we mean the amount and the type of shares being bought or sold. The third important piece of information which must be specified in the contract is the strike price (i.e. price buyer would be paying for the asset when the option is exercised). The fourth item to be specified in the contract would be the expiration date of the option. The fifth item to be written in the contract would be the settlement terms. This means whether the sellers will deliver the real asset or an equivalent amount of cash. And finally, the last piece of information included in the option contract is the total cost to be incurred by the holder to the seller of the option.

Chapter 6: Guideline to a great Stock Investment

Good stock investment is probably the most reliable procedures that a person can use to make money fast and in an easy way. The development in technology has made stock market probably the most trustworthy niches that one may invest in. Individuals are no longer confined to the telephone or other sorts of expensive avenues when doing their business. The internet has taken reliability which makes it simple for individuals to invest in an effective, dependable means. Nevertheless, not all the investors in the stock market get the best from the procedure. Only the experienced and enthusiastic ones obtain the best from the investment.

First of all, you need to conduct before thinking about acquiring excellent stock investments is to determine the market and learn more about it. The principal reason why most of the people do not ever become successful in this lucrative market is as a consequence of stepping into it thoughtlessly. Getting amply trained with the intended niche is the key for you to get a reliable investment. You ought to observe the regular stock investment faults and figure out how to avoid them. This helps to avoid the dangerous faults that can result in falling apart of the business within a short period. The key to making it in the stock market is to acquire more information every day.

The second thing that a person ought to do is to find the most dependable dealer in the market. The brokers are the key tools that assist one in reaping the best from the investment. When the price of the broker is high, most likely the benefits produced will probably be untrustworthy. Likewise, when the agent is inactive or difficult to rely on, the effectiveness of the company will not be worthwhile. It is, therefore, important to seek the services of an excellent dealer to gain good stock investments.

Particular thinking is also an essential factor that impacts the effectiveness of excellent stock investments. Individuals fail to achieve their investment because of inadequate organizing. Stock marketing isn't any different from another enterprise. The planning must be completed, and judgments created so as to reach the best. Deficiency of this awareness has resulted in the crumbling of numerous investments in the industry nowadays. The income produced from the business has to be kept in a separate bank account from similar accounts. This is so to identify the performance. The only portion that one can get is the income; the remainder continues to be with the business which should be self-sustaining.

Lastly, caution has to be taken for good investments. Every single organization has its issues and thus does stocks and shares. Many people seem to manipulate the desperate traders to experience every last coin from them. It is, therefore, important that one takes caution when producing any investment. The best agent needs to be chosen and careful investment created. It is always great to invest a manageable quantity whose damage would not result in monetary disability. Time is the best investment that one can give for a dependable stock investment.

Chapter 7: Trade Exit

In most cases you might already have a system that can help you find a great trading option. You should also already have figured out your maximum loss, just to be on the safe side. What this simply means that you should know early on when is the best time to exit a market that you will not incur so much loss. Because many traders are daring enough to ride the market for as long as they want, or they can predict for it to turn eventually and start giving them the profits that they expect. If you are not yet confident that you can do this, set a maximum loss nonetheless.

These exits are referred to as stops in trading lingo. And there are two types of these stops. The first one is the initial stop, and then there is the trailing stop.

To define the first kind of stop, an initial stop is a point wherein you will exit a trade because you know that if you continue you will just also continue to a loss in that market. If you want to have a different take on it, it also involves some humility on your part. Because you are admitting that you are on the losing end of that trade or market and that it is time to jump ship. This is why stops are necessary for your trade exit strategy.

The other one is called the trailing stop. It is set in almost the same way as an initial stop; based on indicators, percentages and technical. A trailing stop is calculated from the highest price point when you entered a trade. What this means is that your exit point or stop is not at a fixed price as that of an initial stop. It changes or moves as the trade price changes. The Nicolas Darvas system teaches when or how to set up a stop, so you do not make too much of loss.

What makes the trailing stop a bit more confusing or harder to manage and define is that you need to find that balance between the point that you are still expecting to get some profits and up when you need to exit the trade. Otherwise, it may already be too late for you when you finally decide to leave.

On the other hand, the great part with the trailing stop is you can take advantage of the trend for as long as it is in your favor. This way you are minimizing your losses, even if you are just taking in very little profits because of the way the market is trending.

Every stock trading strategies would teach you the importance of having these stops set early on. Before you even become active in a market or trade, you must already predefine your stops so you can avoid losing too much from your activities. Otherwise, when it is time to leave a market, you have no real idea on when is the best time to do so.

Always remember to have the proper trade exit strategy, especially if you are just getting started in the trading field. Even the great traders like Nicolas Darvas understand the importance of these exits. Keep in mind that the best traders always know when to give up on a market to live and fight for another day.

Chapter 8: Important Stock Trading Tools

It's obvious that you can make money trading stocks. A lot of people before you have done this and have enjoyed tremendous wealth and success. Before you decide to start exploring this avenue, however, you should know that there are a couple of important tools that you absolutely must have before you start to trade.

Trade Broker

If you've just started tinkering with the idea of stock trading, it's important to realize early on that you need a broker. You just can't accomplish anything without one. The only ones who can place any trade are brokers so look for a good one before deciding to trade.

The path towards trading stocks for a living would have been extremely easy if you could just go ahead and grab any broker. The thing is, you need to make the right choice to make good profits. Although you will ultimately remain responsible for your decision, your broker choice can still make a lot of difference. If you feel that you need constant good advice, you might want to settle for a full-service broker. Otherwise, a discount service provider would be the best choice for you.

Chart Package

Even if you've never made a single trade in your life, you would know that you need a charting package to move along. Every single person who has been able to make money trading stocks has used a software package.

Picking a tool can be a bit tricky because there are many options. Usually, though, the best picks are those that are old. A ten-year-old tool would be a better pick than a three year old one. This is simply because an old tool implies that it is still in the market mainly because users, through the years, have found it to be of excellent quality. Moreover, with more users around, you are likely to come across more third-party support. This means even if you can't find the answers in the manufacturer's portal, you have many seasoned users to consult.

Trading Plan

A plan or system is by far the most important factor to successfully trading stocks for a living. Without a clear plan to follow, your software and broker will amount to nothing. As the term suggests, a trading plan is simply one that puts order into your decisions. With a good plan, you are supposed to be able to limit your losses to bearable limits and maximize your profit potential by helping you detect appropriate entry and exit points.

Some plans are available online for you to buy and use. It is often more advantageous though to create a plan that is specifically made for you. A custom system is best because it is the only one that will fit your style, preferences and loss tolerance to a tee. Getting a pre-set plan puts you at risk of having to force yourself to accept someone else's rules.

You can't beat trying to make money trading stocks. Before you jump right into the fray, though, you should ensure that you have everything you need to help you succeed. Get your hands on these three tools before you make even a single trade.

Chapter 9: Double your Money in the Stock Market

When you invest in the stock market, you can make money in two ways. Companies may choose to pay dividends to their stockholders. A dividend is part of the company's net income that they pay to shareholders. For example, they could decide to pay 25 cents for every share you own in a quarter. This would mean that if you had 100 shares, they would pay you $25. They usually pay dividends quarterly and are not required to pay every quarter or at all.

You can also make money through capital gains when to own stock. If you had 100 shares of stock that you bought originally for $5 per share, you paid a total of $500. If the price goes up to $8 per share and you sell it for a total of $800, you'll make a capital gain of $300.

This is basically how it works, oversimplified. If a stock is selling for $5, there are 100,000 shares up for sale, and 100,000 shares are being bought or ordered, the price will stay the same because the exact amount of demand is being supplied since it has cost $5. If the there are 100,000 shares up for sale, and 200,000 shares are being bought or ordered, the price will go up because the demand has surpassed the supply.

More people want to buy than are willing to sell. Therefore, the price must go up in order. If there are 100,000 shares up for sale, and 50,000 shares are being bought or ordered, they must lower the price to get more people to buy.

Let's use an example besides stocks. If a department store is selling 30 pairs of jeans for $50 each and they only sell ten pairs after a week, they will need to bring down the price. The price was too high for most people, so now that it is lower, more people will be able to afford it and are willing to pay for them.

If they only put out 15 of the 30 pairs and they all sold within a few dollars, to not run out, they could increase the price so that demand goes down. More importantly, they will be making more money. The same is with stocks, as demand goes up so does price and you will make more money.

Chapter 10: The Importance of Trading Psychology

Why do you need to know about trading psychology? This is for you to understand why two traders, no matter what their skill levels are or the amount of knowledge they know about the market, will always have different results with their trading activities. That even if they have the same stock trading strategy there will still be different endings.

For the purpose of our explanation with regards to the psychological aspect of market trading, let us assume that we have two very identical men who are into trading. It does not matter if you think of them as twins or not, what is important is that they have the same trading background, the same training, the same tools and information regarding the market and even the trend they are interested in. That they both have everything the same when they need to do trading.

Now let us take a leap forward to a few months after our two guys have started with their trading activities. And since they both have everything similar that they need to do their trading (training, tools, data, etc.) it is natural for us to expect that they had achieved the same results. However, as always with anything related to human nature, it is not the same.

One of them ended up making great gains from his trading while the other one simply ended up in the losing end. So how come they achieved completely different results if they both have the same tools, strategies, systems, and information regarding their trading activities?

The answer lies in trading psychology. Because the cause of it all is their individuality after all. They are still different people even if they have the same knowledge and skills in stock market trading. It is, therefore, safe to say that each of them thought differently and acted differently when they had to make a decision with their trading.

As an example of this trading psychology, let us say that both traders were at one point on the same level in the market since they had just started. When the trend started to move, each of them made different decisions. One of the traders decided to stake it and stay with the trend, in the end, he was rewarded with big returns. The other trader, on the other hand, decided to bail out and thought at that time that he would not risk losing in that trade. How exactly they came up with those conclusions is something that is not easy to comprehend.

This is where a trading system would have been very useful, assuming that these guys were not using one. When you have your system, you are expected to follow it as your guide to help you make the right decisions whichever market you may be.

Therefore, the important thing to remember is that for you to succeed in any market, you will have to check on your emotions and decision-making capabilities. It is not enough that you learn to trade even from the best traders. There are certain factors that you will have to deal with yourself.

Chapter 11: Common Investing Mistakes Beginners Make

Whether investing money to the tune of $1000, $10,000 or much more, there are basic investing mistakes that most beginners make. These mistakes can be very costly, so let's look at investing $10,000 and how beginners can do things right.

When investing money, beginners must realize that there is no such thing as a perfect investment. You can't have it all in any one single investment. If you are investing $10,000, you must have your personal financial objectives in mind. What are your priorities from this list: high liquidity, safety, growth, higher income, tax advantages? Be honest with yourself and your financial planner if you have one. Investing money is all about tradeoffs, and what level of risk you are willing to accept.

Of all the investing mistakes beginners make, not knowing and sticking with your financial objectives is the worst. If you are investing $10,000, do you need instant access to your money (high liquidity) in case you have a financial emergency? If so you need a safe investment like a money market fund; and you give up growth, higher income and tax advantages. Otherwise, you could be faced with fees and penalties, or market losses if you need to cash in at the wrong time. For example, you don't want to be forced to liquidate a $10,000 stock investment that's fallen to $5000 just to make your mortgage payments.

Once you have your objectives in mind, get a handle on the investment options that fit your needs before you start investing money. For example, if you are working for a living and investing for retirement, you need at tax break and should consider an IRA or your 401k plan at work if you have access to one. If you are investing $10,000 a year you might want to put half in such a plan and the other half someplace you can get to it without penalties. Lack of liquidity one of the most common investing mistakes beginners make.

Avoid excessive costs and fees. Investing money in stock funds and bond funds to get growth and income do not need cost you an arm and a leg. Investing $10,000 in the wrong mutual funds could cost you $500 off the top when you invest and as much as

$200 or more EACH YEAR for expenses and other fees. This is one of those investing mistakes beginners make that can be costly over time. For example, people invest in bonds to earn a higher income, and over the long-term, bonds have returned about 6% a year. You can't afford to give a third or half of that back in charges and fees. Go with no-load index funds. There are no sales charges to invest, and investing $10,000 can cost less than $50 a year, period.

Investing money successfully need not be a part-time job, but it does require a little ongoing effort on the investor's part. Ignoring the status of their investments is a common investing mistake beginner and many other investors make. Look at your quarterly statements when you get them. Are there charges and fees you don't understand, are you losing money? You can not correct a problem if you don't know it exists.

You can avoid the common investing mistakes beginners make and put yourself in a better financial position. Know your financial objectives and get a handle on your investment options. Keep your cost of investing low and stay on top of your investments. Once you have cash reserves set aside for liquidity, you can start spending money one step ahead of the crowd.

Conclusion

There's a lot of information about investment trading. If this is one area that you would like to explore for yourself, one of the very first points you should settle from the start is what you will be trading. Tackling this is the only way you can take the right steps to isolate the best resources to help you get started.

Several markets are great for investors. Among your best market options are stocks, options, CFDs, commodities, and currencies. If you take a look around at where the top investors are, you might see that many of them have investments in two or three markets. You shouldn't follow the same step as a beginner.

You might think that the best investments are those that are diversified. Most likely, you're thinking that the more diverse your portfolio, the lower your risks of losing. This might initially seem logical since different markets have different risk levels. One loophole to this reasoning, however, is that you will understandably be unable to gain mastery over any market.

Let's clarify things. Investing can get pretty complicated regardless of the market you're in. You need to learn loads of technical terms and processes. Moreover, you also need to build up your instinct for detecting good trades. What this implies is that you need a large amount of time and effort to learn the ins and outs of just one market. Once you dive into wide investment trading, you could lose all you have because you don't have the level of skill and knowledge needed to get you through.

What you should want to know is which market is the ideal one to get into first. Logically, you should start learning the ropes in a market that you are at ease with. You'll find out which market this is if you start reading about each to get a feel for what is easiest for you to learn and understand.

Many specialists would point out that the easy path is to trade stocks first. Obviously, this doesn't mean that stock trading is simple. Among all the markets, though, the stock market is the most clear-cut. Also, you will find that there are quite many excellent resources for you to access and use. There are more than a handful of expert references and tools that you can tap for stock trading to help you make the best investments possible.

There is also a lower degree of risk in the stock market than in any other market. Take note that no one is spared from the possibility of losing a lot in this market. Stock traders, however, do lose less than those in other markets who invest just about the same amount of cash. This is because stocks, unlike currencies, are not leveraged. Keep in mind that high leverage assets can yield huge profits for small investments but also present the risk of huge and quick losses.

Thanks for downloading this book. It is my firm belief that it has provided you with all the answers to your **Investing** questions and you will be a step closer to having financial freedom.

-- *Lance Knight*